I'm
Out
To Change
My
World

I'm
Out
To Change
My
World

Ann Kiemel

**impact
books**

ACKNOWLEDGEMENTS

Our thanks to the following publishers for permission to quote from the following copyrighted songs:

"**God Can Do Anything**". Copyright ©1946 by Singspiration. All rights reserved. Used by permission. Composed by Ira Stanphill.

"**I Will Serve Thee**". Copyright ©1969 by William J. Gaither. International copyright secured. All rights reserved. Used by permission. Composed by Bill and Gloria Gaither.

"**Lonely Voices**". Copyright ©1967 by Hope Publishing Company. International copyright secured. All rights reserved. Used by permission. Composed by Billie Hanks, Jr.

"**Something Beautiful**". Copyright ©1971 by William J. Gaither. International copyright secured. All rights reserved. Used by permission. Composed by Bill and Gloria Gaither.

"**Without Him**". Copyright ©1963 by The LeFevres. International copyright secured. All rights reserved. Used by permission. Composed by Mylon LeFevre.

dedicated to jan, my sister . . .
she makes me believe in love

Table of Contents

The Agnostic

I whipped into a small gas station,
"Uhm, sir,
    could you fill it up please?
        I'm kind of in a big hurry.
            I'm on my way to the airport."

                    "Oh, you are, are you?
                    Where are you going, lady?"

"Oklahoma City."

                    "Going to visit friends there?"

"No, sir, I'm going to speak."

                    "What do *you* speak about?"

And I stuck my head out of the car window
    and I said,
    "Hi, sir. My name is Ann.
        Did you really want to know?"

                    "Yeah, that's why I asked."

"Well you see, sir,
    Jesus Christ is the Lord of my life.
        He laughs with me
            and cries with me
               and . . ."

                    "I'm an agnostic, Ma'am."

"Wow! An AGNOSTIC?
A real AGNOSTIC?
I don't meet many of those.
Uhm, tell me sir,
do you have any problems?"
"Yeah, I've got a lot of them."
"Tell me one."
He squatted down beside my window
and looked in as he said,
"I'm so insignificant."
His face was sober
and his voice was so bitter
as he said,
"I'm so insignificant."
"Sir, me too.
I'm just an ordinary girl
but Jesus adds a lot to my life."
And I began sharing Christ with the attendant
'til the gas started spilling out over the car
and he ran
and grabbed the pump
and washed off the car
and . . .
"Sir, I'm really going to have to go.
I'm afraid I might miss my plane."
Suddenly, I saw this dirty, grimy hand
reaching through the window.
I didn't care if it was dirty—
"Brother,
I'll take your hand.
I'll walk with you
in the name of Christ
I'll love you to Jesus."
He looked through the window at me—
You know, lady,

10

for the first time in my life
you've made me want to believe.
Thank you."
I'm going where He goes . . .
Will you?
And He'll be there beside me.
The love for which He died
Is all I need to guide me.
And He's my gold . . .
Is He yours?
And my silver brightly shining . . .
He writes the music
on a quiet summer morning.

I'm an ordinary girl in a big world
but I'm going to change it—
God and I
and love.
"Yes sir, I'll walk with you.
And you, ma'am.
And you."
You and I together,
we can make it.
Believe with me in the world where you live.
I need you,
and God needs you.

God Is So Good

I was flying to Florida just recently
and I was seated next to a surgeon.

"Sir?
You know what, sir?
I know you would find this hard to believe
but do you know what I did at 5:00 A.M.
this morning?
I just happened to awaken out of a dark sleep,
and sir, I just lay in bed and cried.
Because you see, sir,
I am a Christian
and Jesus is the Lord of my life.
And sir,
I'm so glad that He walks with me
and that He even chose to invade my life
and live in my humble apartment
and laugh with me
and cry with me
and understand me.
Sir,
do you know what I did at 5:00 this morning?

I just slipped out of my bed
on my knees
just to weep out my love for Him.

"I love Him, sir.
He is more than just a great God high above,
He's the Lord of my life.
He puts His hand on my shoulder
and He wipes my tears.
I hear Him laughing when I laugh,
I feel His silence when I am silent."

The surgeon turned and shook his head and said
"Young lady,
some people might laugh at you,
but I'd like to have that kind of faith in God,
How did you find it?"

"C. S. Lewis says,
'Either we say Jesus Christ is a great man,
or we fall on our faces and say,
He is the Lord.'
I have problems,
as a matter of fact,
in my own private world
in a way I can't share.
I am walking the loneliest road I've ever walked,
I didn't know a desert could be so dry
but I love Him,
I really love Him.
And I know a simple girl named Ann doesn't walk alone,
a great big Lord has chosen to invade her life
and walk with her.
He is so good."

God is so good.
God is so good, God is so good.
He's so good to me.

If you have eyes to see
or a little boy next to you
or if you have someone to call a friend
if you felt the warm sunlight in your face today
or saw the blue sky and laughed
you must know what it means to sing
'God is so good.'
If you know what it feels like to laugh with God,
to have fallen flat on your face
and have Him reach out
and say I still love you, take my hand;
to feel Him lift your guilt,
to ease your pain,
to have Him soothe your tired,
worn, broken heart,
then you must understand how good He is.
So sing with me,

God is so good.
God is so good, God is so good.
He's so good to me.
I love Him so,
I love Him so, I love Him so.
He's so good to me."

15

Taxi Driver

It was in the summer
    and I got into a beat up old cab in Miami Beach
    and asked the old cab driver
    to take me to another hotel.
    It was hot
      and every window was rolled down.

And I asked him,
"What is the one word
    that describes your life?"
                       "Can I give you two?"
                             he said.

He was old and gnarled,
    about as beat up as his cab.
"Yes," I said.
    "What are they?"
                 "Bored
                   and unhappy."
"Sir,
    why are those the two words
that describe your life?"

"I don't know.
I guess 'cause
I got nobody in the world."

"Nobody, Sir?
No wife, no children, no family?
No one in the whole world for you?"

"No."

"Tell me, Sir,
how did you get to be an old man
and have nobody?"

" 'Cause I never got a good job
and no woman wanted me."

"Sir,
can I sing you a song?"

"Sing?"

"I don't have a very good voice,
but I know you'd like my song."

"Just a minute, please."
He rolled up his window.
Then he nodded at me.

And I began to sing:

**Something beautiful,
something good.
All my confusion
He understood.**

**All I had to offer Him
was brokenness and strife.
But He's making something beautiful
out of my life.**

"Sir,
do you know who I'm singing about?

Jesus Christ, He's the Lord of my life.
    He laughs with me
and cries with me—"
                        "I'm a Jew."
"Sir, He'll walk with you.
    He'll laugh with you.
He'll be your friend."

And just then we pulled under the portico of the next hotel
    and I was fumbling in my purse for my money
        when I saw this old hand reach out
            and I let loose of the money in my purse.
    I reached out and took his hand
        almost afraid to look him in the eye
            because I didn't know what he would say.
    I lifted my eyes to his
        and he was crying.
                "Lady,
            when I got in this old cab tonight
        I was the loneliest person in the whole world.
    I never heard anyone talk like you talked tonight
                and I want your God.
            He and I could ride together."

And I crawled out of that old cab
    knowing that somewhere in Miami Beach
        an old, gnarled, wrinkled man
    drives a beat up old cab.
        But he doesn't drive alone.
    And I can hardly help but sing
        when I know that the eternal God
    is willing to invade an old cabbie's life
        and love him.

Homesick GI

I boarded a plane in San Antonio
> and I had been speaking to 500 teenagers that week
>> and I was exhausted.

I asked the stewardess,
> "Would you mind if I had a seat by myself,
>> I'm just so exhausted."

She said she understood
> and she put me by a window
>> with the whole row cleared of everybody else.

I looked out the window,
> I was going home,
>> and I love to go home.

I was going home knowing that 500 teenagers in Texas
> believed with me for my world.

> > And the sky was yellow and orange
> > and the sun was setting.

I knew there were other people on board
    but I just started to sing:
                    This is my story
                    this is my song.
                    I really felt like singing.
                    Praising my Saviour
                    All the day long.
                    Oh Jesus,
                    I want to sing about you.
                    I want people to hear me
                    sing about you.
                    This is my story
                    this is my song.
                    Praising my Saviour
                    All the day long.
And out of the clear blue sky
    I heard a man's voice say,
"Uh, ma'am,
    do you hate to leave San Antonio?"
            And I turned around
                and there was a young kid
            and I wondered where he came from.
            "Uh-uh,
                I don't mind at all.
            Do you sir?"
"Yes, ma'am, I do."
            His face got sober.
"You see, I just got back from Viet Nam
    about two weeks ago
and I saw two of my best buddies
    murdered before my very eyes.
And then when I got home
    my wife was gone
and all the family I have left

is right here in Texas
and I'm going back to war."
                    "I'm sorry, sir.
                            I didn't know your world
                            was so ugly."
"Lady,
        was that you singing
a minute ago?"
                    "Yeah, it was."
"Lady,
        what makes you so happy?"

And I turned and looked him in the eye.
                    "Sir, my name is Ann.
                            Do you really want to know?
                    You see, I'm a Christian
                            and Jesus is the Lord of my life.
                    He laughs with me
                            and cries with me
                    and walks lonely roads with me.
                            And, sir,
                    He and I are out to change the world.
                            And, sir,
                    He can change your world."
The tears began flowing
        down that young GI's face.
                    And he looked at me.
"I never knew a God like you have ·
        How do you find Him?"

And I opened my purse
        and pulled a card out
                and wrote a prayer on it.
        Not a special prayer,

a prayer off my head,
         I just wrote it on a card
and handed it to him.
            "Sir, if you'll pray this prayer
            and mean it,
            Jesus will become your friend
            and Lord of your life."
And that's all that was said the entire flight
      and I had taken a nap
      and the plane was on its descent.
Suddenly, he leaned over to me and said,
"Ann, excuse me,
      I know you're tired and everything
but I wanted to tell you something.
      I wanted to thank you.
I prayed that prayer
      and I don't feel alone anymore.
And Ann, I think God and I—
      we can make it."
                  And I reached out and took his hand.
                  "Sir, you and God,
                        you can make it.
                  Anywhere and through anything.
                  Remember this:
                  God and I,
                        we're walking with you."

And I deboarded that plane
      and there were thousands of people in the airport
            but I really believed,
                  that I had the most important mission
            of any of the people hurrying about me
                  because I had changed my world
                  in just a little way.

I'd reminded a broken, lonely GI
that Jesus lived and loved
and would walk with him.

Lonely eyes.
I see them in the subway.
I do—we have subways in Boston you know.
People burdened by the troubles of the day.
Men at leisure
but they are so unhappy,
Tired of foolish games they try to play
Lonely voices fill my dreams.
Do they yours, Sir?
Your voice sounds lonely, your face looks empty.
Sir, take my hand. I'll walk with you.
I'll be your friend.

Ordinary Days

**Something beautiful
something good
All my confusion, He understood
All I had to offer Him,
was brokenness and strife
But He's making something beautiful
out of my life.**

Sometimes people say,
"Ann, I want to speak like you.
I want to do like you.
I want to be a dean of women at a college.
What do I do to be like you?"
And I look back over my life
and I remember being that little girl
with my father on long walks
and him saying to me,
"Remember just this . . .
It pays.
It pays to serve Jesus."

I grew up in Hawaii
and don't tell me what prejudice is.
I know.
I was one light face in the middle
of several thousand dark faces on my campus.
I cannot remember one night in my junior high years
that I did not cry myself to sleep
and wonder why my face couldn't be dark, too.
I wondered why Hindus and Buddhists
had to laugh at my God.
I wondered why friends laughed behind my back
because I was a foreigner.
And all through my junior high years,
I kept saying,
"Daddy, why does it pay to serve Jesus?"
And my father would say,
"Hang in there.
It pays."
And so many mornings, I'd say,
"Mom, I don't want to go to school today."
And she'd push me out the door
with my brother and sister and say,
"Don't you kids know
that life is made up of ordinary days
when there's no one to pat you on the back?
When there's no one to praise you?
When there's no one to honor you?
When there's no one to see how brave and noble you are?
Almost all of life is made up of ordinary days.
And it's how you live your ordinary days
that determines whether or not you have big moments.
Get out there
and make something of your ordinary days."
And I'd stumble out the door in tears.

And I still remember the last day in my large high school.
My sister and I were on the platform to receive little awards
    but a lot of kids could make A's.
    And we were getting scholarships
        but whoever heard of Northwest Nazarene College?
And when they would make the announcements,
    the students would give slight applause
    and they would go on.
    And then the principal called Jan and me.
    He said,
        "We're Hindus and Buddhists,
            but these two girls came
        and brought their God to our campus.
        They've changed our world."
    And I can only remember the applause
        and that it never seemed to end.
I was speechless.
    I can remember the tears dripping off my chin.
Inside I was whispering
"Daddy you were right.
    Through the thousands of ordinary days
        when I wanted to give up, it paid.
    It pays to be true.
    It pays to follow Jesus."

And I went to college
    and faced good days and ordinary days.
But when I was a junior,
    it came to me.
        "Ann, either you are going to follow
            Jesus Christ to the end
        or not follow Him at all."
    After all,
        I was an honor student.

I was becoming somebody on campus.
I had big dreams.
I had high hopes.
Follow Jesus to the end?
What if I never had a dream come true?
What if nothing special ever happened?
Nothing I ever loved ever came my way?
Would I follow Jesus to the end,
if everything I loved was taken away?
Would I make that kind of decision to follow?
For you it might have been an easy decision.
For me it was six long months—
ugly months—
of struggle.
"Jesus, how can I?"
'Til I remember kneeling by the couch
in the TV room
and piling into my hands all that I loved
and knowing what it meant for the first time,
"Yes, Lord, from now to the end I will follow you."
Yes, Lord
to anything
anytime, anywhere.
Yes, Lord—if you'll go with me.
That was really the turning point in my life.
I chose on my own
to follow Jesus to the end.
I don't know what it will mean to follow to the end.
I have a feeling it's a long road,
and there are a lot of mountains.
But I love nothing better than adventure,
and I'm ready to climb.

Spinach And Dreams

I was a sophomore in college
and my sister and I had to work our way through
and someone suggested we work at Birdseye.
The pay was terrific, they said,
and with the other scholarships and all,
if you could get on at Birdseye
you could pay your way through college.
And Jan and I said,
If they'll just call us,
we can make thousands of dollars.
They said, of course,
that the turnover among girls was high,
most girls last one night.
But Jan and I said,
"We're tough,
we can make it."

And when the foreman called and said we had the job,
we thought it was the biggest event in history.
We had heard stories about my Dad—
how he worked his way through school.
We were going to do the same.

31

Every night—
from 6:00PM to 6:00AM.

The first night
we put on our freshly starched white jeans and sweatshirts,
fixed our hair just perfect
and headed to work.
We could hardly wait—
$1.65 an hour!
The first thing they did
was put a hairnet on us that ruined our hairdo
and had a big bill on it that said BIRDSEYE.
The second thing they did to us
was stand us by a moving belt
of cold, wet, spinach.
I like nearly every vegetable in the world,
but spinach, I can't stand.
And the supervisor said we were to sort out the bad spinach
and leave the good spinach on the belt—
all night.
That was our job.

By midnight
I didn't know which was good spinach and which was bad
and I was too scared to ask
and hated it all.
So I pulled spinach
as if I really knew what I was doing.
And I was sick of spinach juice in my face.
The machinery was so loud
I didn't think I could stand it another minute
and we had six hours to go.
I was shivering from the cold
and I began to sing

every hymn I could think of
that had the word "victory" in it.
No one could hear me it was so noisy.
I sang my way through the night.
At 6:00AM the next morning,
my jeans were green
my sweatshirt was green
and I had spinach juice on my face.
And my sister and I stumbled home
and into my parents' room
and fell across their bed sobbing,
"Daddy, I don't care if I never have another pair of shoes.
I don't care about another new dress.
I don't want a college education.

Daddy, you won't make us go back, will you?"
All our parents could do was laugh—
we looked so pathetic.
My father said,
"Go to bed.
You'll feel better when you wake up."
I felt lousy when I woke up.
But I did go back to BIRDSEYE.
My sister went back east to school
but I worked the whole summer.

On the last night of the summer crew
the foreman of the crew came up to me.
"Ann, you're our longest term female employee."
"Really," I said.
"Yeah.
You must really be poor."
"Sir, you're right.
I'm very poor.
"But that's not why I stayed on this job.

I'd rather be poor.
But God and I have big dreams, sir.
　　And with big dreams you have to keep on,
if you give up in one little area,
　　the next big thing that comes up
you'll want to give up in that, too.
　　And with big dreams, sir,
　　　you just can't give up."

Three Rows Every Sunday

So I went to teach school in Kansas City
 and never forgot that lesson.
You know where I lived in Kansas City?
 One room, upstairs, no heat,
  no air conditioning,
   a bed that sagged
  and a lamp stand.
 I was teaching school every day
  and every night I would awaken suddenly.
   "Jesus, I'm scared.
That sophisticated-pseudo-sophisticated campus
with those pseudo-sophisticated teachers,
 and the anti-religious principal.
 How can I share You with them?"

Those were the loneliest days of my life,
 but I remember one day when I scooted my chair back,
  it was between classes,
   and went out in the hall
  and I began to grab kids.
  "Do you go to church anywhere?
  I've got something exciting to tell you.

Would you come to church with me?"
The first Sunday my little Ghia was packed.
The next Sunday it was, too.
On the next Sunday I asked my church for a bus.
And I began to fill it with students.
On Sunday morning it wasn't an unusual sight
to see me coming down the aisles with 25 kids,
the drop-outs,
the most popular.
And we'd fill up three rows every Sunday.

And every Sunday morning
some little old lady would come up to me and say,
"Honey, have you talked to the principal about this?"
"Well, no, I haven't.
It's only on Sundays,
and I haven't really said anything."
But one morning I said,
"This is the reckoning.
I know I'm going to be persecuted like Paul.
This is the end of my job,
but I've got to tell him."
And I walked into the principal's office.
I was scared to death of Mr. Wallace.
"Sir, you gave me accelerated students
and I've crammed knowledge into their brains,
but it takes more than that to make a person.
I believe that because I'm a Christian, sir,
and I also believe that without Christ
there is no meaning to life,
and so, sir,
I need to tell you that every Sunday morning
I've been bringing a bus to school and picking up students
and taking them to church with me.

I'm out to change my world
and I don't know where else to begin.
He looked up and a smile spread across his face.
"You know,
you can't believe how many phone calls we've gotten.
Parents who can't do a thing with their kids
think it's the greatest thing that ever happened.
I never knew a teacher who could spend five days with kids
and want to spend a sixth with them.
But if you want to, it's okay with me."
I stumbled out the door
with a sense of shock and surprise and excitement.
**I'm going where He goes
and He'll be there to guide me.
His love is all I need
to guide me.**
*No, not the perfect words,
not the very right situations,
not the very right opportunities,*
**And He's my gold,
And my silver brightly shining
He writes the music on quiet summer mornings.**

Ann

Every afternoon
I would park in front of the Milican High School campus.
   It was the biggest campus in Long Beach.
   And every afternoon I would park there
      when the kids got out of school
      and I would just watch them.
   And every afternoon I would whisper,
         "Oh Jesus,
      I don't know how I can get on this campus
         but Jesus, it's part of my world."
      And the kids looked so aimless
            and so empty
            and so lonely
                  and I wanted to share my Christ with them.
One afternoon
I remember literally
      putting my arms up around the steering wheel
         and burying my face and sobbing.
               It seemed so hopeless.
      The policies for any kind of a Christian touch
         on a campus in Southern California
            are so strict.
               And I didn't think

that there would be any way
that I actually could get on the Milican campus
—and help change it.
But it suddenly came to me one day—
why didn't I go to the principal?
I mean he was the head of the school
and he had the say about everything—
why didn't I confront him?
Well, I didn't know a thing
about Milican's high school principal
but I called the secretary and asked her
if I could see him.
"Well, you know he's a very busy man
and I really don't think he can take an appointment,
but I'll check with him."
She came back to the telephone and said,
"Well,
he says he'll see you this afternoon.
How will that be?"
And I said,
"Just great."

I didn't know what I would say to him
but I walked into his office and said,
"Hi, Mr. Wood.
My name is Ann.
I live in your world—
Everyday I drive by your campus
and I look at your students.
You see, Mr. Woods,
I'm a Christian.
Jesus Christ is the Lord of my life—
He laughs with me
and cries with me
and walks lonely roads with me.

Oh, Mr. Woods,
I've been a teacher with accelerated students
and I know
it takes more than cramming knowledge into kids' brains
to make their lives fulfilled.
Mr. Woods,
I know this sounds ridiculous.
I know what your policies are on this campus.
I know you haven't even allowed
Campus Life
or Youth for Christ
to come to campus.
But Mr. Woods,
I will sweep floors,
I will clean rooms,
I'll do secretarial work—
I'll do anything you have for me to do
if you'll just give me a chance
to live
and breathe
and share
with the students on your campus."
I couldn't believe it
when he looked up and said,
"Well, Miss Kiemel, you're very convincing.
You know, I've never heard anyone
with that kind of positive approach before.
As a matter of fact,
I do have an idea.
Once in a while,
if I'm really impressed,
I'll offer a forum on campus.
You could come on campus
and hold a forum for the students.
I know how busy you must be

41

and I can get the print shop
to make up all the posters
and do all the advertising.
How would that be?

I stammered out that that would be wonderful
and walked out of his office
with a sense of awe
and simple joy
because of a giant of a God inside me
and because I, an ordinary girl,
am linked to an extraordinary God
and there is nothing that is impossible.

That night
the student president of Milican High School called,
"Is this Ann Kiemel?
Ann Kiemel, who are you?
Are you some kind of angel or something?
I'm Mike so-and-so,
the student body president at Milican.
Do you know Mr. Woods, our principal?"

         "Well," I said,
         "I met him this afternoon."

"Are you trying to tell me
that Mr. Woods is allowing you on campus
to hold a Christian forum?
I don't believe it.
I can hardly get in to see him.

    He allows nothing with the word 'Christian'
      stamped on it
        at anytime
        or anywhere
          on his campus."

"Well, I don't understand it.
But all I know
is that he told me
I could do it.
He even volunteered
to have all the publicity
done for me."
"Would you come over to the campus tomorrow?
I want to meet you.
I really do believe you are an angel."

The next afternoon I met the student body president
and I shared my Christ with him
and my hope for the world.

I brought all my teenagers together and said,
"Mr. Woods has given us this opportunity,
what shall be our theme?"
And we prayed,
and we dreamed,
and we thought—
what would be our theme?
Finally one of the kids asked,
"Why don't we just plaster ANN all over campus
and create such a spirit of inquisitiveness
that they come to find out who ANN is?"
Well, it scared me
but it did seem to be kind of a good idea.
I mean it was unique and original.
So I called Mr. Woods
and he agreed
and the print shop went to work.

I have never been more scared—
before or since in my life

as I was that afternoon
on the way to Milican High.
It was the roughest campus in Long Beach—
would they walk out on me,
would they boo,
would they throw tomatoes?
I didn't know.
Nervously,
I walked on campus
and mingled with the students
who had just gotten out of class.
They looked hard and indifferent.
When I walked into the huge auditorium
I couldn't believe it was nearly packed.
The student body president
asked if he could introduce me
and he did.

I started just like I always do.
"Hi, I'm Ann.
I'm a nobody.
I live in a big world.
But I'm out to change it.
You see, I'm a Christian.
I believe in Jesus Christ.
He's the Lord of my life.
He laughs with me
and cries with me
and walks lonely roads with me.
And He'll walk with you."
And I began to share with them
how they could find Jesus Christ
and how he could become their Lord.
I couldn't believe it—

no one moved,
no one laughed.
They sat there
and they listened.
I began to see kids wipe tears from their faces—
there was a stillness,
a quietness,
a presence.
When I finished,
I knew prayer wasn't allowed on campus,
but we had gone that far,
how could we stop?
So I asked them to bow in prayer.

Afterwards they clustered around me,
those who couldn't get to me
reached out and touched me, sobbing
"Thank you, Ann."
"For the first time in my life, you've brought me hope."
"Ann, I've never heard anything like that before."
"Your God became mine today."
"Ann, thank you."
I stumbled out of that auditorium
and across that campus—
my back was a little straighter,
my head tilted a little higher,
and the God inside me was a little bigger.
I'm going where He goes . . .
I am, anywhere
And He'll be there beside me.
The love for which He died . . .
not sophistication, or perfect words
Is all I need to guide me.
And He's my God . . .
He really is,

Is He yours?
And my silver brightly shining.
He writes the music on a quiet summer morning.

That's my story.

I'm going where He goes—
out into the world
of lonely people.
"Sir, can I take your hand?
Or yours, ma'am?
Can I walk with you?
Can I laugh with you
and cry with you
and love you to Jesus?"

John

You just can't stop love.
It crushes barriers.
It breaks and builds bridges.
It finds a way through.
It never gives up.
It's hard work.
It listens.
It walks ten extra miles.
It's something you do.
Jesus did it for me.
He died to set me free.
He lives to share my life with me
and I go to His
and my
people
and love wins.

One kid,
his name was John,
walked around with his head down all the time.
He never looked you in the eye,
and if you ever got close to him,

he shuddered.
One day John wasn't there,
    and I said to the kids,
"Let's try an experiment.
    Let's really love John,
I mean,
    really love him.
As we've never loved anyone before.
    Let's just see what love can do for John."
He was the most inhibited, insecure kid
    I had ever seen in my life.
From that moment on
    we asked Jesus to help us love John.
Every time he came into a room,
    everyone wanted to sit by John.
We sent him letters.
    We wrote notes during the week.
        We stopped by to buy him a coke.
After six months of loving John
    the kids started to get tired.
        "Gee, Ann,
            you don't know what it's like to love John.
        You call him at home
            to see how his week is going
        and he says 'M-m-m, OK.'
            John, you say,
        I really have been thinking of you
            and I love you
        and he just grunts."

But I'll never forget the morning
    we were all gathered together
        and suddenly
            John smiled.
We had never seen John smile.

He really smiled.
And two weeks later when he laughed out loud
it nearly blew our minds.
No one wanted John to notice
but they were all trying to signal me—
"Had I noticed?
John laughed,
he really laughed."

Three weeks later
his mother, who was a non-Christian—
the whole family was non-Christian—
called me and said,
"Ann,
last weekend we were in the mountains camping.
John is 16
and I haven't seen him cry since he was five.
But he started to cry and bawl and sob.
And after four hours
I was almost frantic
and I asked him why he was crying like this.
All he could say over and over was
'I'm such a failure, Mom,
I'm such a flop.'
And finally I said,
'It's that church you're going to,
they're not treating you right.'
And he said as he shook his head,
'No, no.
It's my only hope, Mom.
They love me over there.' "
And she said,
"It seemed like the minute he said that,
the minute he came out and shared that with me,
he began to dry his tears,

and he straightened his back
and held his head up.
And it's strange,
he's never been the same since.

And in the group
he began to laugh alot,
he began to share in conversational prayer when we prayed.
He began to bring a friend on Sunday,
and two friends the next Sunday
and he became the best softball player we ever had.
For the first time in his life
he had the courage to play ball.

Love changed John's life,
just love.
You can do one of two things in your world.
You can build a wall
or you can build a bridge
to every person you meet.
I'm out to build bridges,
are you?
Come and build bridges with me.
Sir,
can I take your hand?
Or yours ma'am?
Can I pick you up little boy
and hold you in my lap
and kiss your cold face
even if it's dirty?
Can I love you to Him?
Can I love you so much
through thick and thin
until you learn

that Jesus really cares for you?
Can I love you until you feel hope for your world
and your tomorrows?
That's my hope.

That's my story
And it can be yours.

The Architect

I started in Long Beach with 88 teenagers.
I didn't know anything about being a youth director.
I just prayed one simple prayer,
"Jesus, You called me.
I am nothing
but You are everything
and I only make one request—
that You do things
so big
so unusual
that people will be able to look on
with a sense of awe
and say it is too wonderful—
only God could have done it."

And then I didn't know where to begin
but I told those 88 kids
if they would just learn to love each other,
Jesus would trust us with the whole world.
But love is hard work
and it took a lot of months
for the big, tough football players to learn to love
but they learned.

And in a year and a half
    we had Sunday School in three sessions on Sunday.
And we had Sunday School on Tuesday afternoons
    for the neighborhood guys who couldn't get in on Sunday,
      and three more sessions on Wednesdays,
      and a club on Thursdays.
        From Sunday to Sunday
          in a year and a half
        we had four hundred teenagers
      just because 88 kids learned to love each other.

You tell me love doesn't work—
        and I don't believe you.
Every time I went on a trip to speak
      those kids prayed for me—
      twenty-four hours a day
      around the clock—
because they were out to change the world.
    They'd say,
      "Ann, we can't fly with you
      but we'll stay here and pray."

An architect in our church walked up to me
    and he was crying
    and he said, "I want to tell you something.
    A couple of weeks ago I got up early—
      at 4:30 A.M.—
      to fly to Panama
and I saw the light on under the door of my son's room.
      Now, Rick's a sharp kid
      but we can't get him up
      even at 7:30 A.M.
    And here it was 4:30
    and the light was on in his room.
    I bounded across the hall and threw open the door

and I couldn't believe it—
there was Rick kneeling beside his bed with his Bible open—
                                                                praying.
'Rick, what is the matter?
    It's only 4:30.
Are you having some special problem?'
                            'It's Ann,' Rick said.
                'She's in Detroit this weekend
                and I pledged to pray every morning
                        between four and five while she's gone.
    You know, Dad, we're out to change the world
                and when you change the world
                        you've got mountains.' "
                            And the architect said,
            "I walked out of his room
            and closed the door
            and forgot my trip.
    I went into my room
    and fell on my knees by my bed
    and buried my face in the sheets
                    and wept—
                'Oh, Jesus,
        I don't love you enough.
            I don't care enough.' "

Miracle

I guess my faith for the world
    began when I was in Long Beach.
        I had read in the Bible about David and Paul
    and I began to pray,
        "Jesus, the world is so big and I am so small.
    Jesus, I want to see a miracle, too.
        Jesus, please bring a miracle into my life.
    I know you are big enough
        for my world today."

I was Director of Youth in Long Beach at the time
    and I presented it to my teenagers.
        "Do you really want to change the world?
        Do you really want to?"
            And they did.
    We had learned to love each other
        and had a fellowship of several hundred in the group.
So I said,
    "Okay, let's begin to pray about a miracle.
I mean we read about them in the Bible all the time,
    but how many of you kids
        really believe that God is big enough

to do what he did with twelve ordinary fishermen **today?"**
None of us seemed to really believe that.
"Alright, this is February.
This summer, let's take the first two weeks of July
    and during those two weeks
        we're going to pray together
          and laugh together
      and walk the streets together
        and share Christ together.
And the last day of those two weeks is July 11th.
    I know this is just February,
but somehow I believe that that should be our day.
    Starting now we'll begin praying for our miracle.
When you expect big things from God
    I believe He says, 'Are you ready?'
      July 11th is our miracle day."

You see faith is kind of like jumping out of an airplane
    from 15,000 feet up—
if God doesn't catch you—you splatter.
    But how do you know unless you jump?

February came and went.
    March came and went.
        Whenever we had a big party planned
          the kids would say,
      "Ann, if we're expecting a miracle,
then maybe we should cancel the party,
    and go to the church to pray."
        So we didn't have one party in four months.
          I'd plan them
             and the kids would cancel them,
      and every Friday night
    we would kneel around the altar of our church.
Under the great cross

kids would pray simple prayers like,
"God, I'm an ordinary kid,
but I want to change the world.
God, do a miracle for us,
so we'll know You're big enough."
And we began to share with each other
that with every miracle comes a sacrifice,
that every great dream has its price,
that this kind of dream is costly.

April came and left and the kids began to believe.
My football players,
big, tough ball players
came to me and said,
"Ann, we just wanted to tell you
that we got together and decided—
well, we decided that, you know . . .
The coaches told us that if we weren't in practice
the first two weeks in July,
I mean those two weeks are really important,
that we couldn't play first string in the fall.
But we told the Lord
that even if we couldn't play first string
that the coaches would have to count us out
for those two weeks,
because we were expecting a miracle.
We're gonna try to change our world.
We just wanted you to know
that you could count on us."
I had parents come to me.
"Ann, don't you understand.
We've been planning our vacation for a year.
And now John says he can't go,
he's got to be here.
And those are the only two weeks."

I said, "I don't know how to explain it to you.
I feel inspired about it.
We just want to know we serve a miracle God.
And those two weeks are important!"
We prayed,
   we sacrificed,
      we believed,
         we began to give up.

I didn't know much about miracles
   so I got my Bible and read about Esther.
      She was a woman and so was I.
         She wanted to save her nation
            and so did I.
   I didn't know much about miracles
      so I read about hers.
   It told about how she fasted for three days
      before she went before the king.
            I'd never really fasted much
               but if she could, I could.
      I told the kids that for the next three or four days
         I'd be fasting
            and if they wanted to join me
                     they could.
         It was funny,
            the second day I began to get phone calls.
"Ann.
   How are you feeling?"
         "Good."
"Pretty weak?"
            "No, I'm feeling okay."
"Have you fainted yet?"
It was in June,
   the day after I had ended my fast,

the phone rang in my office.
                "Ann, this is so-and-so
        I'm the campaign manager for
                a well-known politician in California
                who is running for Congress.
He's a Christian and I understand you are too,
        and I understand you do a lot of speaking.
We need as much exposure for him as possible
        and I was wondering if you could
                give him some of your appointments.
        I'm sure you're interested
                in getting a Christian in Congress."
"Well, yes Ma'am.
        I certainly am.
        That sounds exciting.
        I'll see what I can do."
And just as we started to hang up, she said,
                "By the way,
                        he is a very close friend of Pat Boone's.
                Now, I can't promise you anything
                        but maybe, by chance,
                Pat could come to your city sometime.
                        He's really very busy
                but maybe I could work with you and . . ."
"Thank you very much," I said,
        and hung up.
And the minute I put down the receiver it seemed to click.
        What if Pat Boone was to be our miracle?
        He could reach more people in one hour
                than we could find.
                        What if he came to our world?
        I ran into Dr. Gilliland, our pastor.
"I've got it!
        I've got an idea.

What if Pat Boone was our miracle?"

Stoic Dr. Gilliland looked up from his notes,

"Do you know how much he charges?"

"Well, no, not really,

I hadn't thought about it."

"Try five to ten thousand dollars.

I've already checked."

Five to ten thousand dollars,

I couldn't even see the figures.

All I had gathered was maybe two hundred.

And when I turned to leave, it clicked.

"That would be the miracle, Dr. Gilliland.

He could come for free."

"Ann, would you please quit dreaming?

I walked back

and went through my speaking book

and picked out some good appointments

and then did something that

I didn't tell the kids about until weeks later.

I decided that there was no way I could touch Pat Boone

unless it was through this politician.

I knew I'd have to see this Congressman face to face.

I'd have to share my story with him

or he'd think I was crazy.

I called the campaign lady back.

"I have some real exciting appointments for you.

But I've been thinking,

how can I support a man running for Congress

if I don't even know him?"

"I don't know," she said.

"I just don't know if I could

if I've never met the man.

So I couldn't give you my appointments

unless I can meet him."

"Well now, he's a very busy man.
And I'm just a campaign worker,
I've hardly seen him myself."
"Well, I'm sorry.
But that's the deal.
Either I get a personal appointment
or I can't give up my speaking engagements."
Well she was very huffy
and said that she'd have to see
and hung up.
I could hardly believe it
when she called back.
"I can hardly believe it
but he says he'll see you.
How about tomorrow about 11:00?"
"Great. Would you like to go with me?"
"Oh, I really would," she said.
"What is your address?
I'll pick you up."
I picked up the campaign worker I hardly knew
and headed for his office.
I didn't know a thing I was going to say.
There was only one thing I knew;
a miracle is something only God can do.
And so I said,
"Jesus, if Pat Boone isn't to be our miracle,
help me to really flub it."

And I walked into this plush office
with all these impressive men standing around
and he dismissed them and asked us to sit down.
And I don't know why but I just said,
"Tell me why you are running for Congress?"
And he began his memorized speech about pornography

and the poor legislation today
and he was just rolling along
and right in the middle I interrupted him.
"Sir, do you believe in miracles?"
"Miracles?
Did you say 'miracles'?"
"Yes, sir.
I'm asking you
because you haven't a chance
of winning this election.
You have a very strong opponent.
I didn't have the slightest idea who his opponent was.
He kinda laughed.
"I guess I better believe in miracles."
"Sir, I do.
I believe in miracles,
but I never really saw one just for me.
And I have some good speaking appointments lined up for you,
but I have an idea.
I understand you're a good friend of Pat Boone's
and Pat Boone could reach more people in my world
in one hour
than I could find in a year.
I know Pat Boone charges five to ten thousand dollars
for any personal appearances.
And we couldn't pay him a cent."

By that time the little campaign lady was green.
She wished she didn't even know me.
She wished she hadn't come.
What kind of a fanatic was I?
First, I asked him if he believed in miracles
and then I asked if he could get Pat Boone for free.
I got all ready for him to laugh.
But he didn't.

He just casually pulled out his date book.
"Well, Pat and I are very good friends.
We keep each other's schedules,
and so I kind of know what his summer schedule is.
Let me see here.
Ann, I hate to tell you this
but I see only one date all summer
that Pat would be available
and it's a Saturday
and you probably wouldn't want a Saturday
but the only free day he has is July 11th.
July 10th he flies in from the Orient
and July 12th he takes his family to Europe
and well July 11th is it."

I didn't tell him that God had told me 6 months before
that July 11th was to be our miracle day.
I just looked up very solemnly and said,
"That would be a wonderful day.
Do you think it would be possible?"
He said,
"I'll see what I can do."
And I started out of his office.
"Ann, just a minute.
Ann, I'm a Christian but I'm a politician
and I almost forgot until today
that without God I am nothing.
Thank you for reminding me."
"Sir, you and I
both have miracles coming.
Could we pray together about them?"
And he cried and I cried
and we shared our Christ together.
And I walked out
and the little campaign lady staggered after us.

And I rolled down the windows of my Ghia
and headed down the freeway for home
and somehow in the deepest part of my heart
I knew a miracle was about to be born.
And I began to sing the two songs that were our theme
during that entire time.

Without Him I can do nothing.
Without Him I'd surely fail.
Without Him I'm just a drifting
Like a ship without a sail.

And with the wind blowing in my face
and laughing with the God of my life,
I began to sing.
God can do anything.
Anything,
anything.
God can do anything by faith.

I marched into Dr. Gilliland's office
and told him in no uncertain terms
he was about to see a miracle
and to just be ready for it.
I never mentioned Pat Boone to my teenagers
because I knew a miracle was something only God could do.
So I wasn't sure that was to be it.
But my kids prayed
and we sacrificed
and the first week of July went by.
We laughed together
and cried together
and walked the hot streets together

with perspiration dripping off our chins.
We wore little cards with just two words on them.
"Ask me."
And we'd walk up and down the streets of our city.
"Excuse me, sir.
See my tag?
Well, just ask me sir."
"Ask you what?"
"Ask me what the most exciting thing
in my life is, sir?"
"What's the most exciting thing
in your life?"
"That Jesus is my friend.
He laughs with me,
He cries with me
and walks lonely roads with me."
And on the street corners
and in restaurants and parks,
everywhere we went that week
we shared Jesus, the Lord of our lives.
Monday of the second week came.
I had not heard a word from anyone—
the candidate or Pat Boone.
And Saturday was our miracle day.
I had never mentioned Pat Boone to the kids.

And on Monday
I felt led to write Pat Boone a letter.
I knew he got thousands of letters
but I stuck a piece of paper in the typewriter,
and typed something like this:
Dear Mr. Boone,
Hi! I'm Ann.
I believe in a big God and I thought maybe
you built your world around a big God, too.

67

You could reach more people in an hour
than I could find in a year. Could you
come for free? Just for an hour? To share
your Christ in my world?
If not, God has something better.

Good-bye King Boone,
Ann (Esther).

I sent it special delivery,
    I thought that might have a greater impact.
Monday went by
    and Tuesday went by
        and Wednesday night came.
    Everybody in our church was looking at me.
"Ann, I was young once.
    I dreamed big dreams once.
    But Ann, you can't put teenagers on the line like that.
        You shouldn't make them think
            that they can really change the world . . ."
On Wednesday night I said,
    "Jesus, this is my last act of faith.
    I'm going to call my brother."
You see, my brother has never been a Christian.
    Thirty-one years of age,
        he wasn't a Christian when he was five,
            he wasn't when he was 12 or 21,
                he's never been a Christian.
    He wears custom-made clothes
        and buys custom furniture
            and has an impressive job.
And I said,
        "Jesus, I'm going to call my brother long distance
            and tell him that I'm expecting a miracle.
            And if there aren't any such things,

then there is no hope at all."
And I called him,
"Fred, my kids and I,
        we're expecting a miracle
and Fred, you know what it might be?
        I think Pat Boone's coming for free."
                "Baby, if you want Pat Boone
                        I can get Pat Boone.
                The Vice President of Paramount
                        is one of my friends
                and Pat Boone would do anything for him.
                        I'll call him for you.
                All I have to do is pick . . ."
"No, Fred, no.
        Don't you understand?
A miracle is only something God can do."
                "Well, I'm here to tell you Baby,
                        it'll never happen.
                You'll never get Pat Boone for free."
And I hung up the phone
        and I went to the window
                and I shoved it up
                        and the cold air blew in my face
        and I looked out at the thousand stars.
                "God, I've heard about miracles all my life
                        and I've read about them in the Bible,
                but God, I'm just an ordinary simple girl
                        and the world is so big.
                God, how can I, a simple girl,
                        and a simple group of teenagers,
                how can we change our world today
                        if you're not a big God for us.
                God, no one seems to understand,
                        but I believe,
                        and I'm expecting a miracle."

"You know, Ann, it's Thursday
        and the miracle is Saturday.
Do you think we ought to set up the sound equipment?"
                "What do we need sound equipment for?"
"Well, I don't know.
        If it's going to be a miracle,
then it'll probably be pretty big
        and we ought to get ready for it."
                "Alright," I said, "I'll take care of it."
Another kid raised his hand.
"Ann, we've been praying and sacrificing
        and giving everything we've got
for seven months
        and day after tomorrow is the big day
and Ann,
        have you heard anything?
Is anything in the air?"
                "No, I haven't heard anything."
"Maybe we ought to go into the sanctuary
        and remind God we're expecting something."
                "Well, "I said, "it's almost lunch.
                What about lunch?"
He said, "I'll pray through lunch."
                "Allan, what about you?"
"I'm not hungry at all, Ann."
                "Jeannie?"
"I'm headed for the sanctuary."
                "Steve?"
"Who cares about food?"
                I said, "What if supper comes
                        and there's no reassurance?"
"We'll pray through supper."
                "And then what?"
"We'll pray all night if we have to.

God's got to be a big God
or we don't have any hope. Ann.
We're heading for the sanctuary."
And they stood to their feet in silence
with tears on their faces
and went to pray.

We hadn't been in the sanctuary more than five minutes
when the secretary called me to the phone.
I walked to the door and she said,
"Ann, it's Pat Boone.
He's on the phone."
"Oh, no," I said,
I never talked to a celebrity.
I'm not sure what to say."
And I went down the hall
and picked up the phone.
"Mr. Boone?
Is this really you, Mr. Boone?"
"Yes, it is, Ann.
I just got your letter.
I'm holding it in my hand.
Ann,
I never read a letter like yours.
I never knew a girl who
has that kind of faith.
Ann,
Shirley and I get in late tomorrow
and we fly to Europe Sunday,
so Saturday, the 11th, is my only free day,
but if it will work for you,
we'll come on Saturday."
"Oh, Mr. Boone, I don't know what to say.
That would be wonderful."

He said, "Would you mind
                if Albie Pearson,
            the baseball player,
                came with us?"
"That'd be great."
And I hung up the phone
    and for the first time in Ann Kiemel's life,
        I knew that it was no ordinary God
            who walked with me.
        It was a giant of a Lord,
            and he and I—
                we could change the world.
And I ran out and I said,
        "He's coming! Pat Boone's coming!"
            Every secretary in the office,
                and Dr. Gilliland himself,
                    were running to keep up with me.
        They were behind me in a steady stream,
            as if I were the Pied Piper.
I ran into the sanctuary.
        The kids knew nothing about Pat Boone
            but I went bounding in and there they were—
                all over the altars,
                    all over the platform,
                        crying.
        I heard one kid just say this
            "God, don't worry about me.
                I'm believing."
I said, "Listen you guys,
            it's happened.
                Our miracle, it's happened!
                He's coming.
        Pat Boone is coming to us for free
            Saturday morning at 10:00."

72

He can reach more people in our world in an hour
   than we can find in a year."
And the kids stood to their feet
   and we gave God the loudest, biggest standing ovation
      He's ever had.
         And then, one by one,
               my kids started getting down on their knees
            and one of the girl's picked up her guitar
         and with tears running in a steady stream
            she began to play
               and look up at the big cross
                  that we had prayed around for hours.
Without Him we can do nothing
Without Him we'd surely fail.
Without Him we'd be drifting,
   Like a ship without a sail.

   But God can do anything.
      anything
God can do anything by faith.

Saturday morning came
   and needless to say everyone was excited.
      All the newsmen had said
         the deadlines for Saturday were past
      but Pat Boone had never been to our city
         and they were breaking the deadlines.
They had publicity everywhere,
   they had it on TV,
      they had it on radio,
         they had it in the newspaper.
Saturday morning came and the place was packed.
   The aisles were lined.
      There were people seated row by row in the foyer

73

and there were people seated inside the altars.
Church people?
No, people from our world.
People who didn't know Jesus.
Lost people,
hungry people,
lonely people.
And Pat and Shirley whipped up in their little Rolls Royce
and Albie Pearson crawled out of the back seat
and we went into the office to pray
and Pat and Shirley buried their faces and wept.
And Pat just kept saying,
"Ann, show us how to find that kind of faith."
And Dr. Gilliland was saying,
"We better go,
it's ten o'clock and they're waiting."
And Pat and Shirley didn't budge.
"Ann, we want to change our world, too.
How can we find
that kind of faith?"
When we got to the platform
it was my job to introduce Pat Boone.
And I walked to the platform
and I said,
"I am awed and moved today
to be able to introduce to you
my big God.
Pat Boone isn't our hero today,
A big God is.
And that place,
packed with hundreds and hundreds of people
stood to their feet and cried and applauded
and somehow God's spirit spread through
and when it was all finished

I calmly said,
"And now I introduce to you,
Mr. Pat Boone.
You ask those teenagers in Southern California
if they believe in a big God.
You ask them if they are afraid to dream big dreams,
if they feel hope for their world.
There is no question in their minds.
And people look at me and say,
"Ann, do you?"
"Yes, yes."
Though I walk through darkest valley
God, I know that to change my world
there are going to be some dark valleys,
but you've seen me through the dark valleys yesterday.
Though the sky be cold and gray.
Do you like cold, gray skies?
I don't
But there'll
be some for me tomorrow.
There's one for me today.
But God and I,
we've made it through the cold, gray skies yesterday.
We'll make it tomorrow.
Though I climb the steepest mountain
Do you know that dreams are made of mountains?
God, now that I've just conquered a mountain
do I have to climb another one?
Ann, don't you know?
Don't you know
that you've got to keep climbing mountains to change your world?
But like a lamb who needs a shepherd by his side,
I'll always stay.
Give up?

Give up the dreams in my world?
Never.
Not ever.
God and I and love—
we're out to change the world.
God and I and love.

Black Knit Cap

I had been at Long Beach two years
    when I got the call to be the Dean of Women at Eastern Nazarene
    College
I remember saying:

"Uh-huh, Lord
Dean of Women?
I mean,
every dean of women I know is 70 years old.
And she wears her hair on her head in a bun.
And Lord, I'm barely 26.
I don't want to be dean of women.
Boston?
On the other side of the world?
I don't know a soul in Boston.
I don't have one friend on the East Coast.
Dean of Women?
Give up 400 teenagers
that I have laughed with
and cried with
and arm-wrestled with?
Leave them now?"

And I can still remember the few days before I left
When I told my teenagers I was leaving
    half of the boys
        even the rough, tough football players
            stayed home from school on Monday.
One mother said,
John's in his room.
    He's been crying all day.
He's never been like this before.
    What should I do?"
                I said,
                "John's motto is 'Yes, Lord!' too.
                He understands.
                He'll make it."

And I can remember going to the gate to catch my plane.
    People thought I was some kind of celebrity
        there were so many people there to see me off
        I'm sure they were wondering.
    They didn't know I was just ordinary Ann
        except my teenagers,
            "Yes, Lord!" was their motto, too.

I can still remember as I walked through the gate
    I heard a voice.
"Ann, Ann?"
    When I turned around it was Jim.
        Jim was a junior high boy
            who had been won the year before.
        He wore a little black cap.
            It was his whole identity.
    He took his little black cap off
        and handed it to me over the gate.

"Ann,
hang this somewhere back there.
    Put it on a peg someplace
so that when you're back there
        and we're clear out here
you'll know God and I
        are still changing our world."
    And I tucked that little cap under my arm.
                    "Ann."
                It was one of my high school boys.
            He unzipped his jacket and pulled out a carving.
            "Ann, take this with you, too.
        It's pretty special to me,
                but I wanted you to have it,
            because I never want you to think for a minute
                    that because you're in the east
                    and we're in the west
                        that God and I'll stop dreaming.
            If you're on the East Coast
                    and we're on the West Coast,
                we ought to flip this world pretty fast.

And I was crying as I boarded the plane
        and the stewardess said,
"You must really hate to leave."
        And I looked at her.
            "I do.
                I love those kids down there, but . . ."
                I know where I'm going
                and I know who's going with me . . .

New Neighborhood

I moved to Boston to a whole new world
    of big old houses on a neighborhood street
        and I was lost and frightened.
      An ordinary girl walking through a very big desert
        and a very big world.
      But I am a simple girl who doesn't walk alone—
        a great God has chosen to invade my life.

A girl who lived below me was a nurse
    and she found Christ.
        And there was another girl who lived next door.
        Her name was Barbara.
    I never told her I was a Christian.
    I just tried to love her
        and waited on Jesus to open the door.
One day she knocked on my kitchen door and said,
                "Ann."
        She was crying.
         "Ann, just tell me one thing.
          You are always so happy.
           What is it that makes you so happy?"

"Well, Barbara,
        I've been wanting to tell you.
    The most exciting thing in my life
        is that I chose to follow Jesus.
    No one makes me,
        I chose to.
    It was the most personal decision of my life
        and I have chosen to follow Him
    because I know it pays.
        And because He loves me
    and love makes all the difference."
                        "Ann,
                            how can I find Him?"
            And at the kitchen counter
                in my little apartment
                    Barbara, my neighbor,
                        found Him.

    A month later she moved out
        and another girl moved in
            and I couldn't wait for my first night home.
        I ran over and knocked on her back door.
    "I just wondered.
        Do you go to church anywhere?"
                        "No.
                            I'm not exactly the church type."
    "Oh, I see.
        I didn't mean to be offensive.
    I understand
        but I have a very exciting church
    and usually I'm out of town on Sundays
        but I was wondering
    if some weekend
        when I'm in town
    if you would want to go with me?"
                        "Well, I guess so."

The next week she knocked on my door.
"Is this one of your weekends at home?
I just want to go to church with you."
And she did.
But that wasn't when she found Christ.
It was one night when I knocked on her door
and sat at her kitchen table with her.
"Jesus Christ can make a difference in your life, Linda.
He'll be your friend,
He'll walk with you,
He'll be your Lord,
even as He is mine."
And in tears at a kitchen table
she accepted Him.

Two months ago she moved to Florida
and now a couple lives in her apartment.
I'm so excited.
I'm out to love them to Jesus.
And I will.
You watch,
you wait,
you'll see.
Give up?
Never.
My aim is victory.
No matter how hard the road.
I have a giant of a God
and He and I in love can do it.

The Sidewalk Sweeper

A little old lady was sweeping the sidewalk
    and one day I drove up,
        and I was in a big hurry,
            and I looked up and said,
                "Isn't this the most splendid day?"
And she kind of looked up and nodded.
                "I have the most exciting God in me."
            And I ran on up the stairs
            and into my apartment
            and then it came to me
                that she lived next door.
        It was the wealthy little elderly lady
            that lived next door
                that was sweeping the sidewalk.
I had almost forgotten that she was part of my world.
                "Jesus—
            would You give me a chance
                to win her to You?"

It was about six months later
    when I started to run into my apartment
        and the little elderly lady stepped out.

                                         "Honey."
                            And I looked over and said
                               "Oh, how are you?"
She said,
"I've been watching you every day for a week.
I just returned from the hospital.
   I was lying on the bed dying
      and in my sub-conscious state
         I heard the doctor tell my family
            that I only had a few hours to live
            and I wouldn't make it through the night.
Lying there I thought of all the funerals I've ever been to
and I began to say,
         'Oh, God,
         if You will just help me
         talk to that girl next door before I die—
         there was something about her
         that makes me think she's got something I need.' "
And then she went on to say
      how the doctors couldn't believe
         that she lived through the night
      and how every day since she had come home
she'd been watching for me.

"How did you know about my God?" I asked.
"Do you remember the day
   I was sweeping the walk
      and you told me you had
         a wonderful God inside you?
      There was something about the way you spoke—
I had never heard anything like that before,
         and I wanted your God, too."
"What is your name?"
                                   "Mrs. Nelson."

                       86

"Mrs. Nelson,
would you like to go into your apartment?
It might be easier to pray there.
Would you like for my Christ to become your Christ, too?"
And she began to weep
and we went into her elegant apartment
and with her weeping and bent over
I began to share with her
how my Christ could become her Christ.
How He could laugh with her
and cry with her
and walk with her
even as He walked with me.

It was beautiful when I walked out of her apartment
and realized I had changed my world in a little way
because I had reminded an elderly lady—
who lived next door in my world—
that Jesus lives and loves
and would walk with her.

June

One day a girl came in on her bicycle.
She had another friend with her
    and this friend's father was president of the city college.
    And she was an agnostic.
        But I loved her anyway.
    I wrote poetry with her;
        I laughed with her.
    I arm-wrestled with her on the floor;
        I jogged with her;
        I rode a ten-speed with her.
    I shared Jesus with her everytime I got a chance.

She would call me some nights
    and in the middle of a conversation
        she would slam the phone down in my ear.
    I don't know how often the phone slams in your ear
        but I didn't exactly appreciate it.
    I mean after all,
        she was the one who called me.
But I loved her.
    Although, I really shouldn't say so
        because sometimes I really wanted to give up.

And sometimes I really wanted to smack her in the mouth.
But Jesus in me loved her.
Through thick and thin.

And then one day seven months later
the phone rang.
She was sobbing and crying,
"Ann,
I don't know how to tell you.
But today at school,
in an unexpected, obscure moment,
it came to me—
God has to be.
Because no one in my life loved me the way you loved me.
If anybody can love me through my moods
and the drugs
and all my mess the way you loved me,
there has to be a God.
Ann,
in an obscure moment today
I found him."
Just about a month ago,
I got a letter from June.
She has Bible clubs everywhere.
Jesus is Lord of her life.
She's out to win her family to Jesus.
She believes.
Just because somebody loved her
through thick and thin
and you see, you can't stop love.
Love finds a way through.

Buster

A little boy knocked at my door one day.
    He was dirty and hot
        and he had wads of newspapers under his arm.
        "Would you like to buy a paper, lady?"
"Well, what kind of paper is it?"
        "Grit."
"Grit?
    What kind of paper is that?
I never heard of it."
        "Well, ma'am it's a paper I'm selling
        and it talks about . . ."

Well, I couldn't have cared less
    but I looked at him
        and he looked so tired and worn out
    so I said,
"Okay, how much?"
        "Quarter,"
        So I went and got a quarter.
"What's your name?"
        "Buster."

"Hi, Buster.
    My name is Ann.
Doesn't it get pretty hot
    walking these streets every day?"
            "Yeah."
"Pretty tired?"
            "Yeah."
"Buster, I'd like to be your friend.
    And whenever you're out selling papers,
if you get real thirsty
    or real tired,
I want you to know you can come to my place,
        and I'll give you some cold Kool-Aid
and let you sit down in the cool
        and we'll laugh together.
How does that sound to you?"
            "Pretty good."

And so Buster started stopping by my house.
    I guess just because somebody cared about him.
        And he needed someone to care.
One day I said,
    "Buster, take me to your house.
I'd like to meet your family."
        He sort of shuffled his feet.
        "Gee, Ann.
            It's not a very nice place
            and I don't think you'd like it."
"Buster, I don't care where you live.
    I just want to go with you."

He took me to a little shack with two rooms,
    a bathroom and one big room, and
        a father of some 80 years of age.

Buster, his little sister
and his father all lived there.
Their alcoholic mother had deserted them years before
and only dropped in now and then
and the time I met her
she had a big gash across her face
where she had fallen.
I had never been in a place like that in my life.
But I was out to love Buster to Jesus.
He was part of my world
and I really cared for him.
One day Buster said to me,
"Do you like fishing?"
"Well, I guess so.
I mean I'm not a very good fisherman.
I hardly ever go fishing."
"Would you go fishing with me sometime?"
"Sure, I'll go fishing with you.
Where do you go?"
"Well, there's a pretty good drain ditch
up the road."
"Oh, when did you have in mind?"
"How about Saturday morning?"
"Saturday morning?"
I had only one day to sleep in
and that was Saturday morning.
But, after all,
if you love someone you have to make sacrifices.

"What time, Buster?"
"What do you say about 5:30?"
"Buster,
I know the fish wouldn't bite at 5:30.
That's way too early."

"Yes.
That's the very best time—
5:30 in the morning.
That's when they really bite."
"Are you kidding me, Buster?
Fish actually bite at 5:30 in the morning?"
"Sure they do."
"Well, okay love.
Come by at 5:30
and we'll go to the drain ditch."
If we were going to a big lake
it would have been more exciting.
But a drain ditch—
at 5:30 in the morning?

He knocked on my door 15 minutes early
and I wasn't out of bed yet.
I jumped into some old clothes
and we headed for the drain ditch.
He had dug a can of fat slimy worms.
When we got there I said,
"Buster, I tell you what.
I'll hold the worms while you fish
'cause I really don't know a lot about fishing.
You fish and I'll hold the worms
and maybe later we'll switch."
So I seated myself on a cold, hard rock,
holding the can of worms
and Buster went down to the ditch.
It was in his heart.
He wanted me to see him catch a fish.
He was determined—
And he tried.
He'd say,
"Shh."

"Buster, I told you it was too early."
"Shh.
Be very quiet."
So I'd sit there
looking at those ugly worms, praying,
"God,
Please help him to catch a fish
So we can hurry and go."
After a while,
the sky began to get darker and darker
and soon it began to pour.
"Buster, are you sure fish bite in the rain?"
"Sure, they bite anytime."
"Even in the rain, Buster?"
"Yeah,
it's no problem."
And the water began to run in my hair.
I was getting desperate.
"God, will you please hurry up?"
Buster was not leaving without a fish.
Finally he caught one.
And we were both dirty
and wet
and we got in the car.
Now with a fish in the can of worms.
On the way home, I said,
"Buster, are you hungry?"
"Yeah."
"Would you like to stop at a coffee shop
and get something to eat?"
"Wow! You mean a restaurant?"
"Yeah. Nothing special.
Just a . . ."
He thought he'd like that.

It just so happened
        that there must have been fifty businessmen
        having breakfast on Saturday morning.
            Well dressed, sophisticated.
        And we were dirty and smelled like fish.
    And they seated us and I whispered,
"Now, Buster you can have anything you like.
    If you want five eggs
and three pieces of bacon
        then you order it."
            So he did.
                I couldn't believe it.
                    Five eggs and bacon.
And when the waitress walked away he whispered,
            "Ann, I never been in a place like this.
            This must be the best in town!"
    I couldn't believe that either.
        But Buster had never been in a restaurant.
        I loved Buster.
    Everytime the social worker would come to his house
        his father would send Buster on his bicycle to me.
            "Go get Ann.
                I need her down here quick."
    I made all the family decisions.
            I decided what they did with their money.
                I prayed them through the rough times.
            I told the father what to do in every situation.
        He began to lean on me as if I were his eldest child.
            I baked fudge and cookies.
                I'd laugh with Buster.
                    I'd walk with him.
            Buster and I cried together.
Buster would tell me how embarrassed he was of his house.
        And every time I dropped him off

my heart ached.
Did Buster come to Sunday School?
Only about three times in two years.

But you see, I was out to love Buster.
Not if he came to Sunday School.
Not if he did what I thought he should.
Just to love him.
Through thick and thin.
To love him even after I got him a new suit
and he overslept
and didn't make it to church—
To love him anyway.

Buster's in the service now
but I hear from him.
He's about to get married.
"Ann, there's only one person in my life
who ever really loved me.
And God lives in me because you loved me."
Just a simple little thing like loving him
brought God into the life of ordinary **Buster.**

A lot of times you tell people God is love.
And they laugh.
"Are you kidding me?
Do you see where I live?
Did you see my Dad beat me last night?
God is love?
I don't buy it."
The only love people in your world will understand is you.
God and you loving them.
Then they'll believe.

Mrs. Grissom

It was Saturday night
    and I ran across the street to get the vacuum cleaner.
It was late
    and I was tired
        and in a hurry
    and Mrs. Grissom handed me the vacuum cleaner
        and I looked into her tired, old
                                wrinkled face
and I don't know why
    but as I took the cleaner and started to go
        I said to her,
            "Oh, Mrs. Grissom,
            God loves you a lot."
And the tears just began to spill down her face
    and she said,
        "Could you wait just a minute?"
        She went back into her house
            and got a plaque off her wall
            and brought it out.
    It was a picture of weeds—
Just ugly old weeds smeared all over the picture
and underneath all those ugly weeds were these words:

Weeds
Nobody likes weeds.
Nobody carries them in a bouquet
or wears them in a corsage.
But God waters the weeds.
And she looked up,
"You know, Ann,
all my life
I have felt like a weed."
"Mrs. Grissom,
could I pray with you?
I didn't know anybody
went all through life
feeling like a weed.
There are times when I feel like a weed
but I didn't know anybody
felt like a weed all their life.
Really, I just came to get the vacuum cleaner—
but I was wondering
could we just stop for prayer?"

She said she'd like that
and we went into her little apartment
and I said,
"Would you like to hear
a little song
that I sing a lot in a big lonely world?"

I will serve Thee
because I love Thee . . .
You have given life to me.
"So I'm not just a weed
and neither are you
because He gives us life."

Heartaches, broken pieces
ruined lives are why You died on Calv'ry.
"That's why He came, Mrs. Grissom.
Your touch was what I longed for.
"You see He makes flowers
out of weeds."
You have given life to me.
And I prayed with her.
When I finished praying with her
I looked her in the eye,
"Oh, Mrs. Grissom
I love you.
You are
a very special lady to me."
And the tears
began spilling down her face.
"I've never been special
to anyone before."
I picked up the vacuum
and I ran across the street
to my little apartment
and threw myself across the bed,
"Oh God, it's so ironic!
The people who live closest to us
are the ones we overlook,
the ones we fail to reach out to.
Jesus, use me in the neighborhood.
If I am out to change the world,
I'll have to start in my neighborhood."
The next morning was Sunday
and I called the florist at 7:30
and asked him to put together
the most beautiful bouquet
he had ever fixed.

I wanted the flowers
that looked the prettiest
and smelled the best.
I mean the loveliest bouquet he had ever made!
"Well, look lady,
it's Sunday morning.
I barely have my houseslippers on and . . ."
"But sir, you don't understand.
It's for a very special lady
and I want her to know that she's not a weed—
but that she's beautiful."
"Yes, ma'am.
I'll see what I can do."
"Just write on the card—
'Bright Hope'—'Love, Ann.' "
The very next day
she knocked on my door
with tears running down her wrinkled face.
"I never had a bouquet in my house before,
and Ann,
for the first time in my life
I really knew God loved me."
I'm out to change the world—
in love—
that's my hope.

Mark and Eric, 5 and 6

One day while I was sitting at my desk at ENC
the housekeeper of Munro Hall called me.
"Ann, there are two little boys running in the halls
and will you please come over
and get them out?"
You'd be amazed at the jobs a Dean of Women does.
"I'll be right over."

I marched over and there were two little boys,
their shirts hanging out,
their hair in their eyes,
their faces all dirty,
running up and down the halls,
slamming doors
and banging on the walls.
I took them by either arm and told them,
in no uncertain terms,
was I ever to see them in this building again.
In fact, in no uncertain terms,
I was never to see them
in any building on this campus again
or it would mean *"this."*

I didn't tell them what *"this"* meant
but by the look in their eyes
I figured they understood.
Then I took each one by the hand
and marched them over to my office
and sat them down.
"Tell me your names."
"Mark and Eric."
"My name is Ann."
"Oh."
"Can we be friends?"
It seemed like a pretty good idea.
"Now that doesn't mean
that if I catch you in these buildings
it will be less than *"this"*
but I'll make a deal with you.
There's one building you can come to
and that's this one
and only for one reason.
That's to come and see me,
and you can come anytime you like.
Is that a deal?"
They nodded.
"And when you come,
sometimes I'll buy you a Coke."
Now that really was a good deal
and out they went.

The next morning at 7:20
I was running across campus
and I heard someone calling,
"Ann, Ann."
And I looked over
and there they stood,
Mark and Eric.

"What are you doing here?
        It's only 7:20 and it's not time for school yet, is it?"
Their hands were buried in their pockets,
    sleep in their eyes,
        dirty faces and uncombed hair,
            and shirts hanging out.
        "But you said we could come anytime
            to see you."
"Have you guys had breakfast?"
        "No, our mom is a barmaid
            and she hasn't come home yet."
"Well, I've got to run
    or I'll be late for class."
        But I put my books down
            and my purse
                and knelt down on the sidewalk
                and put my arms around them both.
"I love you, Mark and Eric.
    Isn't it fun being friends?
        Come this afternoon and we'll have ice cream."
        It turned out to be the first
            of many ice cream cones.

It was just about a month later.
    I was in the bakery buying coffee cakes.
        The kind you leave on porches of lonely people
            with little love notes on them.
    It was a little love thought
        and I was late and in a hurry.
    They were wrapping the boxes with string
        and I was writing a check
            when out of the corner of my eye
    I noticed a little boy
        with a great big dog.

I really didn't pay much attention
    but I heard the lady say to the little boy
           "Do you want anything?"
  "No."

    My coffee cakes were ready
        and I tore off the check,
            threw my purse over my shoulder,
        picked up my coffee cakes
          and was headed out the door,
      when I stopped.
        "Eric, I didn't know that was you.
           What are you doing at the bakery?
        I know,
           I bet you wanted something to eat."
His hands were in his pocket
        and his face was a mess, he shook his head, "No."
"Then I know, Eric,
        you just wanted to look in the window
           because everything looks so good."
    And he said no again.
        I put my purse down
          and lay the boxes on the floor.
I knelt by Eric and wrapped my arms around him.
      He kept his hands in his pockets
        and his head down.
"Eric, you haven't been here all this time
        just to see me, have you?"
        His head was down
        but you could see this smile break across his face
          and he looked up out of the corner of his eye
        and nodded his head up and down.
"Oh, Eric, I love you."
        And I kissed his dirty face.
"It's my treat today. Let's celebrate 'cause we're friends.

You can have anything you see."
"But I didn't want nothing, Ann.
I just came to see you."

I picked up my purse and cakes
and headed out the door
with Eric behind me
and a big dog behind him.

A little boy without a daddy,
whose mother works in a bar and is gone every night,
a little boy that needed a friend
and in my heart I whispered,
"Oh, Jesus,"
help me to change his world, too."

Chocolate Chip Cookies

Oh God, it's so ironic—it's so
ironic that the people living closest to us are
almost always the ones we overlook and fail to really love—
I was out to love my neighbors to Jesus.
Everyday I would pray—
        "Jesus, what can I do
            to share you with them?"

It was a Saturday night
        and it had been several months of praying
            when I looked up into the cupboard
                and saw a package of chocolate chips.
    Now I'm not a special cook or anything
        but I can make pretty good toll house cookies,
            and I said to myself,
            "I'll bake them some toll house cookies."
And I threw everything together
        and put the cookies in the oven
            and when they were done
                I threw them on a plate
                    and ran downstairs.

"Sir, hi.
My name is Ann.
And sir,
I baked some cookies for you and your wife.
I'm your neighbor from upstairs.
Well, I baked them for you, sir,
because I love you
and I—
well, what I mean is, sir,
I love you because Jesus loves me
and I don't know why,
He just makes me want to love you and your wife."

He looked blank
and shocked
and sort of helpless.
And suddenly I couldn't think of anything else to say
and I felt foolish
and stupid
and sort of helpless, too.
And so I kind of shoved the cookies into his hand
and said goodnight
and tripped up the stairs
and ran in my apartment
and burst into tears.
"Oh, God, I blew it.
I really blew it.
What a ridiculous thing for a twenty-six-year-old girl
to do.
Take homemade cookies to the man downstairs
and tell him I love him.
He'll think I'm weird.
But God, you know what my motive was.
I was trying to tell him, Jesus,

that he is a part of my world
and his wife is
and I wanted to befriend them and love them to You.
Jesus,
can you make something out of this mess?
If you will, God, I promise—
I will never do anything irrational again.
I'll think it through clearly.

For three days I was heartsick.
I mean they didn't tell me they liked the cookies,
they didn't return the plate,
they didn't do anything.
But at the end of the third day
I was running up the stairs to my apartment
when there on the carpet
in front of my door
was an empty plate with a note taped to it.
I've never been so happy to see a plate in my life.
I ran in the door
dropped my books
and picked up the note
and began to read.

"Dear Ann—
Thanks a lot for the cookies.
We never heard anyone talk about God the way you did.
I was in a convent studying to be a nun when I met Mike
and we've wandered from God.
Could you come down
and have coffee with us sometime
and share your God with us?
Thanks a lot.
Mike and Kay."

I see people—
   warm faces,
      a running tear,
         a small child's hug,
            an old man's gnarled grip of love.
Saroyan said,
   "People is all there is—
      and all there was—
         and all there ever will be."

         People—
      that's all that matters to me
       that Jesus be Lord
        and people.

It Pays

My brother who is 33 now
    accepted Christ two months ago.
        My brother, who laughed that God
            could bring Pat Boone to us.
    My brother,
        who had never been a Christian in his whole life.
I had written Pat Boone and said,
        "Would you look up my brother?
            Could you have lunch with him or something?
            Maybe you could reach him
                in a way no one else could."
            That was about three months ago.
And then about two months ago
    at three o'clock in the morning
        my proud, egotistical brother called me,
    "Ann, it's midnight here
        and I know how late it is there
            but I want to tell you something.

I was down on my knees by my bed
and I got down with my face on the rug
and I asked the Lord
to give me somebody tonight.
Somebody to reassure me and tell me
that even after 33 years of sin
that God still loved me.
And then the phone rang.
And you know who it was, Baby?
Pat Boone.
He said he had just tucked Shirley and the kids in
and he couldn't sleep
and he went downstairs
and he saw your letter
that he had kind of forgotten about
and so he felt led to call me
and tell me that God loved me
and he loved me
and could I come Tuesday
to his house for Bible study.
Baby, let me tell you something;
God is love.
I know that now
and you can count on me."

Ask my father if it paid for 33 years to walk the floor.
I used to hear him as a little girl, praying
"Oh God, save my boy."
And today I'm 27 and my brother is 33.
When you hear my brother talk about the Spirit
and you hear him laugh
with the God of his life,
ask my father if it pays to hang on.
To believe in a faithful God.
To hang on.

What is your story?
The story of you.
How big are your dreams.
Your dreams for your world—
for your city.
**"By this shall all men know that you are my disciples
that you love one another."**
And with you and a giant of a God inside you nothing—
nothing is impossible.
I like to sing **"Alleluia"** because **"Alleluia"** is praise.
Thank you Jesus,
thank you, Jesus, for being such a great Lord.
Thank you, Jesus, for love.
Thank you, Jesus, for hope.
You know what?
Love is hard work.
You know something else?
Love never gives up.
I wonder how many people are willing to say,
"Oh God,
I want more love today and tomorrow than I ever had before.
Oh God,
I want greater faith.
I want to believe you're a bigger God
than I ever believed you were before.
God, I'm just one person,
but God you can count on me.
If you'll fill me,
and walk with me,
you can count on me, God."

I'm Out To Change My World

Many of my weekends now are spent in traveling—
     speaking to churches
          and groups of men and women and boys and girls.
And every time I finish speaking I want to celebrate.
     I want to celebrate His love.
I want to celebrate the thousands of ordinary days
     when I thought I was not going to make it;
I want to celebrate the few big moments
     that have kept me going through the dark ones,
          and I want to celebrate hope.
Hope that there's going to be another side
     of this mountain or this desert,
          hope for the doors in my neighborhood
               that I haven't yet knocked upon.

Do you feel like celebrating?
A song I love to sing is "Alleluia."
     Just that one word that means "Praise The Lord."
          Alleluia for warm sun and blue sky
               and a person next to me to call a friend.

117

Do you feel that way?
Let's celebrate together
Do you know what my dream is?
That Catholics, Protestants, Jews can kneel side by side
in back yards and churches
in living rooms and neighborhoods
and believe together that Jesus,
the Christ of our lives, can change our world.

And tonight in my hotel room I turned out the lights
and looked at the lights of a city
and wondered what kind of beautiful things Jesus Christ could do
if you and I joined hands
and let the Lord love through us.
And I prayed for every car that passed
and for every truck that was going up the freeway ramp.
If Jesus could do so much through twelve ordinary men
what could He do through us?
And I wondered about Buster and June,
and the architect and Mrs. Grissom
and the taxi driver and a homeside G.I.
and about you
and I began to pray:
Oh, Jesus, Alleluia.
Thank you
for laughing with us
and crying with us
and walking us to the kingdom of love.
Fill us with your Spirit.
When we're scared give us courage
when we're weak make us strong
when we want to hate give us love and patience.
And may we wrap our arms around somebody
and love them to you.

May we cry with them as you cry with us,
and laugh with them as you laugh with us.
And may they know You by your love in us.
And that you and I and our brothers in love
can change the world.